ALEX
KUSKOWSKI

A FUN AND CREATIVE INTRODUCTION TO FIBER ART

COOL

PUNCH NEEDLE

for KIDS

Checkerboard
Library

An Imprint of Abdo Publishing
www.abdopublishing.com

VISIT US AT WWW.ABDOPUBLISHING.COM

Published by Abdo Publishing, a division of ABDO, PO Box 398166, Minneapolis, Minnesota 55439. Copyright © 2015 by Abdo Consulting Group, Inc. International copyrights reserved in all countries. No part of this book may be reproduced in any form without written permission from the publisher. Checkerboard Library™ is a trademark and logo of Abdo Publishing.

Printed in the United States of America, North Mankato, Minnesota
062014
092014

THIS BOOK CONTAINS
RECYCLED MATERIALS

Design and Production: Anders Hanson, Mighty Media, Inc.
Series Editor: Liz Salzmann
Photo Credits: Anders Hanson, Shutterstock

The following manufacturers/names appearing in this book are trademarks: Fiskars®, Sharpie®, Ultra Punch®

Library of Congress Cataloging-in-Publication Data
Kuskowski, Alex., author.
  Cool punch needle for kids : a fun and creative introduction to fiber art / Alex Kuskowski.
     pages cm. -- (Cool fiber art)
  Audience: Ages 8-10.
  Includes bibliographical references and index.
  ISBN 978-1-62403-310-0 (alk. paper)
1. Punched work--Juvenile literature. 2. Embroidery--Juvenile literature. I. Title.
  TT840.K87 2015
  746.44--dc23
                            2013043074

TO ADULT HELPERS

This is your chance to assist someone new to crafting! As children learn to craft they develop new skills, gain confidence, and make cool things. These activities are designed to help children learn how to make their own craft projects. Some activities may need more assistance than others. Be there to offer guidance when they need it. Encourage them to do as much as they can on their own. Be a cheerleader for their creativity.

Before getting started, remember to lay down ground rules for using the crafting tools and cleaning up. There should always be adult supervision when a child uses a sharp tool.

TABLE OF CONTENTS

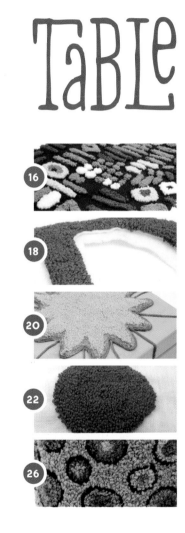

Start Punching

Discover how to make art with a punch needle! Punch needle is a type of embroidery. It is the art of decorating with thread. Punch needle embroidery makes loops of thread to decorate fabric.

In this book you will find a lot of great ideas to get started. They will help you start making punch needle embroidery. An overview of the most basic steps, terms, easy **patterns,** and step-by-step instructions will make learning a breeze. Just turn the page. Start punching it up the fun way!

❖ Tools ❀the Trade ❖

PUNCH NEEDLE

Punch needles come in sizes 1 to 12. Bigger needles hold more thread and make bigger stitches. Some punch needles can be adjusted to different sizes.

Each punch needle has a front and a back. The rounded side of the needle with the eye is the back. The front is the side with the open edge. Punch needles use a threader to put embroidery floss through the needle.

No-slip Embroidery Hoop

Embroidery hoops hold fabric flat. A no-slip embroidery hoop has an extra lip to keep the fabric from pulling out. They come in many sizes. A 6-inch hoop is a good size to start with.

Embroidery Floss

Embroidery floss is a special kind of thread. It comes in many colors. It has six strands twisted together. You sometimes need to separate the strands and only use some of them.

Fabric

You can punch needle any fabric. A popular fabric for punch needling is weaver's cloth. It is made of cotton and **polyester**. It is found at most craft stores.

Almost all fabric has two sides, a front and a back. The color or design on the front is brighter. The duller side is the back.

Patterns

Punch needle **patterns** come with directions. They list the types of thread, hoop, and needle needed for the project. There are tons of fun patterns to choose from!

It's In the Bag

Keep a bag for your punch needle, embroidery hoop, embroidery floss, fabric, and general craft supplies like the ones below!

BAG

BEADS AND BUTTONS

PEN AND PAPER

MEASURING TAPE

SAFETY PINS

EMBROIDERY HOOP

SCISSORS

NEEDLES

GLUE

THREAD

PUNCH NEEDLE

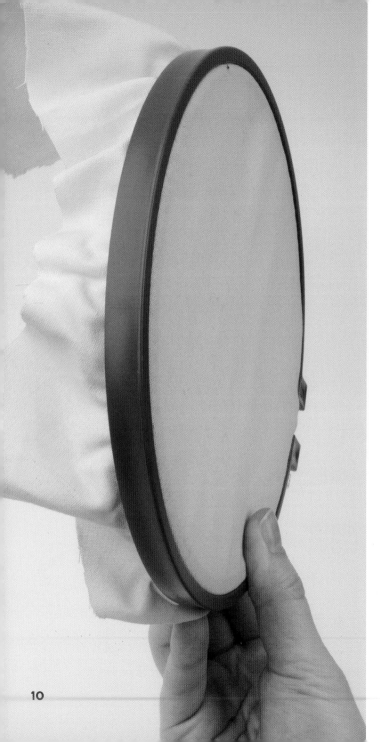

HOOP IT UP

PUT YOUR FABRIC
IN A HOOP!

WHAT YOU NEED

EMBROIDERY HOOP, FABRIC

Loosen the screw on the embroidery hoop. Separate the two rings.

 Lay the fabric front side up over the inside ring. Center it over the ring.

Press the outer ring over the inner ring. Squeeze the fabric between the rings.

Make sure the fabric is flat. Tighten the screw.

 The fabric must be at least 1 inch (2.5 cm) larger than the hoop on all sides.

❧ Basics ❧

HOLDING THE NEEDLE

Face the front of the needle in the direction you are stitching.

Hold the needle straight up and down.

Threading Tips

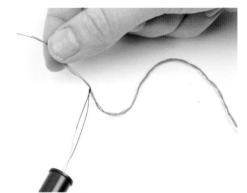

Stick the threader up into the punch needle through the tip. Push it through the punch needle handle until it comes out the top.

Thread embroidery floss through the threader where it sticks out of the handle. Pull the threader back out of the punch needle. Remove the floss from the threader. The floss should be sticking out both ends of the punch needle.

Stick the threader through the eye of the needle from back to front. Thread the end of the floss through the threader. Pull the threader back through the eye. Remove the floss from the threader. About 2 inches (5 cm) of floss should stick out of the eye. About 2 inches (5 cm) of thread should be out of the eye.

STARTING UP

GET GOING WITH
THESE DIRECTIONS!

WHAT YOU NEED

EMBROIDERY HOOP,
FABRIC, PUNCH NEEDLE,
EMBROIDERY FLOSS,
THREADER, SCISSORS

Put the fabric in the embroidery hoop. Thread the punch needle. Press the needle down through the fabric. Press until the handle touches the fabric. Lift the needle but keep the tip of the needle touching the fabric.

 Move over one needle width. Press down again. Continue lifting, moving, and pressing. This creates loops of thread on the opposite side of the fabric.

 Stitch the outline of a rectangle. Then fill in the center.

Always fill in shapes in rows. The rows should be close together. Change colors and make more shapes.

FINISHING OFF

Keep your stitches from **unraveling**. Knot the end of the floss near the fabric. Cut off the extra floss.

PRINTED FABRIC JOURNAL

WRITE IN A
JOURNAL AS UNIQUE
AS YOU ARE!

WHAT YOU NEED

NOTEBOOK, PATTERNED
FABRIC, MARKER,
EMBROIDERY HOOP, PUNCH
NEEDLE, THREADER,
EMBROIDERY FLOSS (IN
COLORS MATCHING THE
FABRIC), SCISSORS,
PLAIN PAPER, MEASURING
TAPE, CRAFT GLUE

 Trace the front of the notebook on the back of the fabric. Put the fabric in the hoop. Thread the punch needle. Hold the hoop with the back of the fabric facing up. Find a shape in the fabric the same color as the floss. Fill in the shape.

 Continue filling in the shapes in the fabric with matching floss. Stop when all the shapes inside the traced rectangle are filled. Cut off any long threads.

 Open the notebook and lay it flat on a piece of paper. Trace around the notebook. Add 1 inch (2.5 cm) to each side. Cut out the larger rectangle. Lay the paper rectangle on the fabric. Line the rectangle on the fabric up with one side of the smaller rectangle on the paper. Cut the fabric around the outside of the paper.

Spread the fabric out face down. Fold the top and bottom edges over 1 inch (2.5 cm). Open the notebook. Lay it face down on the fabric. Make sure the front cover is over the rectangle you punch needled. Lift the front cover and put glue on it. Press the cover to the fabric. Repeat with the back cover. Let the glue dry.

 Fold the sides of the fabric over the front and back covers. Glue them to the inside of the covers. Let the glue dry.

DIVA
LETTER PATCH

"D" IS FOR THE
DIVA IN YOU!

WHAT YOU NEED

COMPUTER & PRINTER,
PAPER, MARKER,
MEASURING TAPE,
WEAVER'S CLOTH,
EMBROIDERY HOOP,
#1 PUNCH NEEDLE,
THREADER, EMBROIDERY
FLOSS, SCISSORS, WHITE
FELT, FABRIC GLUE

1 Print out or draw the letter "D" 5 inches (12.7 cm) tall. Lay the weaver's cloth over the letter. Trace the letter onto the cloth. Put the cloth in the embroidery hoop. The letter should be facing down.

2 Thread the punch needle with three strands of floss. Punch the outline of the letter. Fill in the letter. Cut off any long threads.

3 Take the cloth out of the hoop. Cut around the inside and outside of the letter. Leave ½ inch (1.3 cm) of cloth around all sides of the letter. Lay the cloth letter on the white **felt**. Trace around the cloth.

4 Glue the cloth edges to the back of the letter. Let the glue dry. Glue the letter to the letter on the felt. Let the glue dry.

5 Cut out the felt letter.

TIP Try making a different letter. Remember to punch needle it with the letter outline facing down.

19

RaY OF LiGHT BOX

- -

KEEP A BOX
FULL OF SUNSHINE!

- -

WHAT YOU NEED
....

WOODEN BOX, LIGHT BLUE
PAINT, FOAM PAINTBRUSH,
WEAVER'S CLOTH,
MARKER, EMBROIDERY
HOOP, #1 PUNCH NEEDLE,
EMBROIDERY FLOSS
(ORANGE AND YELLOW),
SCISSORS, HOT GLUE
GUN AND GLUE STICKS,
ORANGE THREAD

Paint the box blue. Let the paint dry.

 Trace the top of the box on the weaver's cloth. Draw a sun inside of the shape. Put the cloth in the embroidery hoop. The sun should be facing down.

 Thread the punch needle with three strands of orange floss. Punch needle the outline of the sun. Fill in the sun with yellow floss. Cut off any long threads.

4 Take the cloth out of the hoop. Cut out the sun. Hot glue the sun to the box. Let the glue dry.

5 Glue orange thread around the sun for extra decoration.

21

COLORFUL CIRCLES PILLOW

WHAT YOU NEED

WEAVER'S CLOTH, RULER, SCISSORS, MARKER, EMBROIDERY HOOP, #1 PUNCH NEEDLE, THREADER, EMBROIDERY FLOSS (THREE COLORS), SEWING NEEDLE, WHITE THREAD, PILLOW STUFFING

22

Cut the cloth into two 14-inch (35.5 cm) squares.

 Draw a dot in the exact center of one of the cloth squares.

Draw dots 3 inches (7.5 cm) on either side of the center dot. The three dots should be in a straight line.

 Draw two circles around each dot. Make the inner circles 1 inch (2.5 cm) across. Make the outer circles 2 inches (5 cm) across.

 Put the center of the cloth in the embroidery hoop. Thread the punch needle with three strands of floss. Outline the inner circle. Then fill it in.

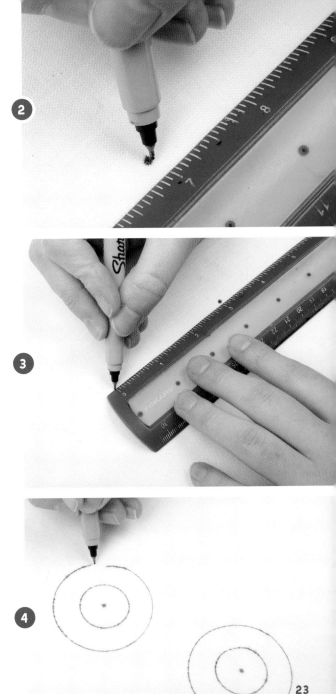

23

6 Thread the punch needle with three strands of the second color of floss. Outline the outer circle. Then fill it in around the inner circle.

7 Center one of the other circles in the hoop. Outline and fill the inner circle with the third color of floss. Outline and fill the outer circle with the first color of floss.

8 Center the remaining circle in the hoop. Outline and fill the inner circle with your second color of floss. Outline and fill the outer circle with the third color of floss.

9 Cut off any long threads.

10 Take the cloth out of the hoop. Lay it on top of the other cloth square. The side with the punch needle loops should be facing down.

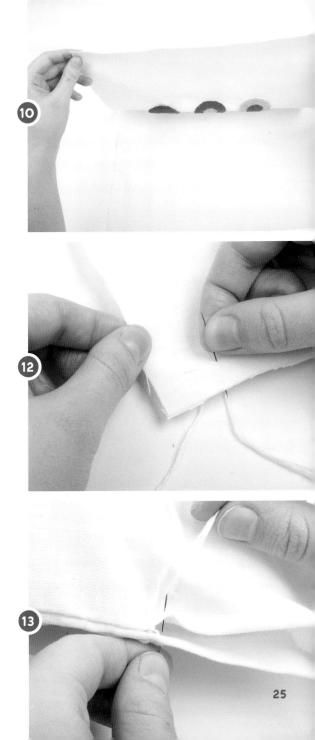

11 Cut an 18-inch (45.7) piece of white thread. Thread it onto the sewing needle. Tie a knot at one end.

12 Starting at one corner, sew the edges of the cloth square together. Sew along all the edges until 2 inches (5 cm) is left open. Knot the thread close to the cloth.

13 Pull the cloth right side out through the opening. Put pillow stuffing through the opening. Fold the edges of the opening to the inside. Sew the opening closed.

CHEERY CUP COZY

WHAT YOU NEED

CARDBOARD CUP HOLDER, MEASURING TAPE, SCISSORS, MARKER, WEAVER'S CLOTH, EMBROIDERY HOOP, #6 PUNCH NEEDLE, THREADER, EMBROIDERY FLOSS (VARIOUS COLORS), HOT GLUE GUN AND GLUE STICKS, FELT, SEWING NEEDLE, THREAD, 2 BUTTONS, NARROW RIBBON

Cut through the side of the cup holder. Lay it flat. Cut off 1 inch (2.5 cm) of the cup holder. Lay the large part of the cup holder on the weaver's cloth. Trace around it. Draw circles inside the shape.

 Put the cloth in the embroidery hoop.

3 Thread the punch needle with three strands of floss. Outline and fill in an inner circle.

4 Thread the punch needle with a different color. Outline and fill in the outer circle. Outline the larger circle with black floss.

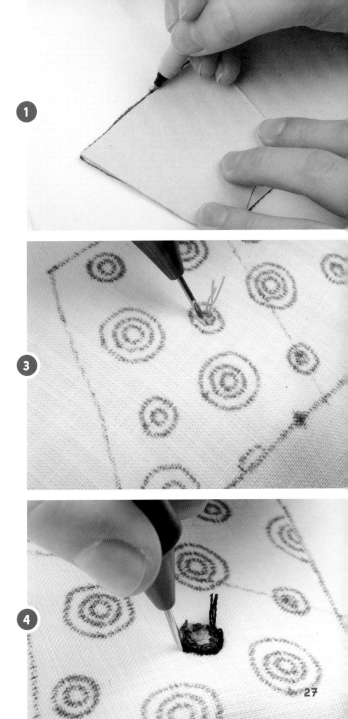

5 Fill in the remaining circles. Use different colors of floss for the inner and outer circles. Outline all of the circles with black floss.

6 Fill in the background with tan floss.

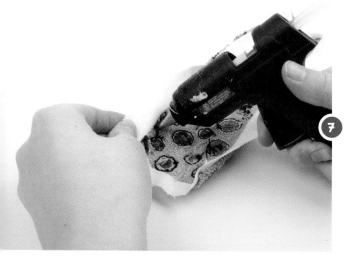

7 Take the cloth out of the hoop. Cut around edges of the cup holder shape. Leave a ½-inch (1.3 cm) border all the way around. Fold the cloth edges to the back. Glue them down. Let the glue dry.

8 Glue the punch needle cloth to the **felt**.

Cut the felt around the punch needle cloth. Leave a ½-inch (1.3 cm) border all the way around.

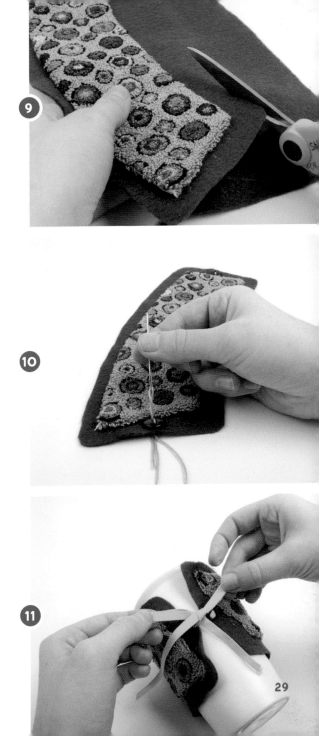

 Cut a 10-inch (25.4 cm) piece of thread. Thread it onto the sewing needle. Tie a knot at one end. Sew one button on each short end of the felt.

Cut a 6-inch (15.2 cm) piece of ribbon. Wrap the punch needle cozy around a cup. Wind the ribbon around the buttons in a figure eight. Tie it into a bow to hold it on the cup.

 This is a great project for using up leftover floss from other projects.

Keep Punch Needling!

Y ou've just discovered how easy punch needle art can be! You can do anything with a punch needle. Make cool stuff for yourself, or gifts for family and friends. There are tons of ways to use punch needle embroidery.

Don't stop here. Explore all the **patterns** out there. Check out books on punch needlework at the library. Or look for ideas online. Get inspired and create your own designs. Try **dressing up** old clothes with new stitches. Make a piece of art. It's all about using your creativity!

GLOSSARY

DRESS UP – to make more attractive or fancy.

FELT – a soft, thick fabric.

PATTERN – a sample or guide used to make something.

POLYESTER – a man-made fiber used to make cloth.

UNRAVEL – to come apart or to come undone.

WEB SITES

To learn more about fiber art, visit ABDO online at www.abdopublishing.com. Web sites about creative ways for kids to make fiber art are featured on our Book Links page. These links are routinely monitored and updated to provide the most current information available.

INDEX